The Greenhouse Effect

Look for these and other books in the Lucent Overview series:

Abortion
Acid Rain
AIDS
Alcoholism
Animal Rights
The Beginning of Writing
Cancer
Dealing with Death
Death Penalty
Drugs and Sports
Drug Trafficking
Eating Disorders
Endangered Species
Energy Alternatives
Extraterrestrial Life
Gangs
Garbage
The Greenhouse Effect
Gun Control
Hazardous Waste
The Holocaust
Homeless Children
Ocean Pollution
Oil Spills
The Olympic Games
Ozone
Population
Rainforests
Recycling
Smoking
Special Effects in the Movies
Teen Alcoholism
Teen Pregnancy
The UFO Challenge
Vietnam

The Greenhouse Effect

by Sharon Elaine Thompson

LUCENT
B·O·O·K·S

LUCENT *Overview Series* OUR ENDANGERED PLANET

LUCENT *Overview Series*

OUR ENDANGERED PLANET

Library of Congress Cataloging-in-Publication Data

Thompson, Sharon Elaine, 1952-
      The Greenhouse effect / by Sharon Elaine Thompson.
         p.   cm. — (Lucent overview series)
      Includes bibliographical references and index.
      Summary: Discusses the greenhouse effect, the consequences of a
warming world, and possible ways to protect the environment.
      ISBN 1-56006-133-2   (alk. paper)
      1. Greenhouse effect, Atmospheric—Juvenile literature.
[1. Greenhouse effect, Atmospheric. 2. Global warming.]   I. Title.
II. Series.
QC912.3.T48   1992
363.73'87—dc20   92-27848
                                                       CIP
                                                        AC

Dedicated to my mother,
Elaine A. Thompson,
and to the memory of my father,
John W. Thompson.
Their love and laughter
have made mine a warmer world.

Contents

Introduction

THE GREENHOUSE EFFECT, a natural phenomenon that keeps the earth warm, is as important to life on earth as food and air. Just as greenhouse glass traps heat for growing plants, atmospheric gases—called greenhouse gases—trap the sun's energy to warm the planet. This is how the greenhouse effect keeps the earth's temperature reasonably constant and maintains a life-nurturing balance of heat and energy. Without the greenhouse effect most life on earth would surely perish.

Yet the greenhouse effect also presents living beings with a challenging, and some say, potentially devastating problem. The earth appears to be warming too much and too fast, and the greenhouse effect may be the cause.

A buildup of greenhouse gases may be trapping too much of the sun's energy and overheating the planet. Most greenhouse gases are created through natural processes such as plant decay. Many of these naturally occurring gases are also produced by human activity. Car engines, for example, spew thousands of tons of the greenhouse gas carbon dioxide, into the atmosphere daily. Some greenhouse gases, namely chlorofluorocarbons, or CFCs, are a human invention that appear nowhere else in nature.

(Opposite page) The greenhouse effect traps the sun's heat in order to keep the planet comfortable for plants and animals.

The human-produced greenhouse gases such as carbon dioxide and CFCs raise the greatest concern among scientists studying the greenhouse effect and its influence on global warming. Human activity adds billions of tons of greenhouse gases, primarily carbon dioxide, to the air every year. As a result, some scientists warn, global temperatures could rise by as much as ten degrees Fahrenheit (°F) by 2050. If this were to happen, the effect on human society could be disastrous. Melting polar ice and glaciers could raise sea level as much as three hundred feet, flooding coastal cities and seaports. Fertile areas could become deserts. Food production could drop, and famine could spread.

Not all scientists believe that the earth is threatened by global warming or that, because of the greenhouse effect, these disasters will befall human society. This is because there is no abso-

Cars spew tons of carbon dioxide into the atmosphere. Carbon dioxide is thought to be a major cause of global warming.

lute undeniable proof that the greenhouse effect is causing global warming or that human beings are increasing the greenhouse effect. Scientists must base their theories on sometimes unreliable historical records and difficult-to-interpret geological or fossil records. Even the computer models widely used for studying the greenhouse effect and global warming are not infallible.

However, many scientists believe a potential problem does exist and they urge immediate action to reduce the greenhouse gases that could eventually overheat the earth. Unlike other kinds of environmental damage, global warming is not reversible, at least not for thousands of years. Oil can be swabbed from the oceans. Lakes and rivers can be cleaned. Smog devices on cars can reduce air pollution. Poisons can be removed from toxic-waste dumps. Global warming, however, may set off a chain reaction. One event triggers another and each new event increases the warming. According to scientists, once a certain point in the chain is reached, human beings will not be able to reverse the damage.

Many researchers believe human beings are getting close to that point now. People probably cannot stop the warming expected to occur because of the greenhouse gases already in the air. According to atmospheric scientist Veerabhadran Ramanathan, the earth may warm by 1°F to 3°F no matter what is done. Most scientists believe, though, that people can work together to maintain the balance in the greenhouse effect and keep global temperatures from rising too much.

1

A Warming World

TODAY PEOPLE TALK about the greenhouse effect as if it were something frightening and unnatural. But it is not. It is the natural atmospheric phenomenon that keeps the earth warm and life on it functioning. The greenhouse effect is the result of a delicate balance between life and the environment. That balance is not fixed. Life on earth can change the environment, and the environment can change life on earth.

It now appears that life on earth is indeed altering the balance that results in the greenhouse effect. The activities of human beings seem to be creating an imbalance in this natural system, an imbalance that could alter the world drastically. To understand the greenhouse effect and why humans have the power to change it, it is helpful to understand a little about the earth's atmosphere.

The birth of an atmosphere

All living beings breathe every moment of every day. People rarely think about what they are breathing unless it is a smoggy day or they are hiking high in the mountains where the air is thin. But the air they take for granted did not come with the earth originally. In fact, 4.5 billion years

(Opposite page) The greenhouse effect helps to maintain the delicate balance between life and the environment. Some fear human activities have altered that balance.

13

ago, the earth had no atmosphere. There was little but the vacuum of space around this molten ball of rock.

As the freezing temperatures of space began to cool the earth, a thin layer, or crust, of solid rock began to form. Beneath the crust, though, still-molten rock churned. Gases from below the surface escaped when volcanoes exploded through the earth's fragile skin. Meteors tore holes in the crust releasing more gases. Those gases were the earth's first atmosphere. They were probably much like the gases spit out by volcanoes today: 64 percent water vapor; 24 percent carbon dioxide; 10 percent sulfur; and 1.5 percent nitrogen.

As the planet continued to cool, the water vapor condensed and started the water cycle—rain, evaporation, condensation, and more rain. Carbon dioxide interacted with the other gases and formed methane and ammonia. There was little free oxygen or nitrogen around, and everything—earth and atmosphere—was bombarded by ultraviolet radiation that poured from the sun.

A change in the atmosphere

These are the conditions in which life is thought to have developed on earth more than three billion years ago. At that time, the bacteria and blue-green algae that made up most of the life on the planet lived in the ocean. There, somewhat protected from the sun's ultraviolet rays, the algae took carbon dioxide out of the water and emitted, or gave off, oxygen into the air.

These primitive plants released so much oxygen that after about a billion years, the atmosphere changed. The oxygen combined with the ammonia, methane, and other gases until the atmosphere filled with nitrogen and oxygen. The air that had once contained mostly carbon dioxide now contained very little. There was hardly any

Lava fountain of a Hawaiian volcano. The gases in the earth's early atmosphere were much like those released by volcanoes today.

methane or ammonia left at all.

This may have been the first case of massive air pollution in the earth's history. It was not good news for the bacteria and blue-green algae. Most of those organisms were used to an atmosphere rich in carbon dioxide; oxygen was poison to them. As a result, most life died. But fortunately, some organisms survived. They adapted and began making use of this strange new atmospheric gas: oxygen.

The abundance of oxygen also created the ozone layer that surrounds the earth today and that is so important to human survival. The ozone, a type of oxygen, blocked out the sun's harmful ultraviolet radiation so that eventually ocean life could crawl out on land without being burned to a crisp.

Other changes resulted from the new atmosphere. Because carbon dioxide made up so much of the early atmosphere and because carbon dioxide absorbs heat, the earth was very warm. When the amount of carbon dioxide in the air decreased, much of the heat trapped in the atmosphere was able to escape back into space. The average temperature of the planet cooled by about 20°F to what it is now—about 59°F. Just enough carbon dioxide was left to keep life on earth comfortable—like plants in a greenhouse.

Holding in the heat

Plants in a greenhouse stay warm even when there is snow on the ground outside because the glass walls and roof trap heat. Similarly, the earth stays warm even though space around it is freezing. The carbon dioxide in the earth's atmosphere traps heat around the earth.

Heat is generated by hot objects, such as the sun, the earth, a kitchen stove, which radiate, or send out, energy. This energy moves away from the objects in waves. The hotter the object, the shorter the wavelength of energy it produces. Cooler objects produce energy with longer wavelengths.

When energy wavelengths strike an object, they can pass through the object, be reflected by it, or be absorbed by it. Much of the sun's short energy wavelengths pass through the earth's atmosphere and strike the ground. Light-colored areas, such as clouds or snow, reflect the sun's energy back toward space. But dark-colored areas, such as soil, plants, and the ocean, absorb the sun's energy. This absorption is what warms the earth's surface.

As the earth warms, it begins to radiate heat. Without anything to stop it, the heat would keep moving farther and farther out into space, and the earth—and everything on it—would freeze. The

The earth retains heat in much the same way the glass of a greenhouse traps heat.

earth's atmosphere, however, prevents this from happening.

Although the short energy wavelengths from the sun can pass through the atmosphere, the heat produced by the earth cannot. This is because some gases in the atmosphere absorb the heat. They hold the heat in the atmosphere, wrapping the planet in a warm, protective blanket.

The ability of the earth's atmosphere to retain heat is called the greenhouse effect. The phenomenon got its name in 1827 when a French mathematician named Jean Baptiste Fourier compared the earth's atmosphere to the glass in a hothouse. The gases that contribute to the greenhouse effect are called greenhouse gases. The most important of these gases is carbon dioxide. Other natural greenhouse gases include water vapor, methane, and nitrous oxide.

When these gases are at their normal levels, they are not environmentally dangerous. Only .03 percent of the atmosphere is carbon dioxide. Methane and nitrous oxide are only found in traces. However, these small amounts are enough to keep the earth warm and comfortable for human beings and the other animals and plants that share the world with them.

Glacial ice cores

Because it takes so little of these greenhouse gases to keep the earth warm, increasing the amounts of these gases in the air could increase the average world temperature. In fact, scientists have found indications that in the past, when levels of atmospheric carbon dioxide rose, world temperatures also rose. Their information comes from ice cores taken from glaciers in Greenland and the Antarctic.

Glacial ice cores can provide a valuable record of climate change over thousands of years. This is

Researchers work with ice core samples. These samples contain trapped air that can reveal temperature levels thousands of years ago.

because snow, compressed over many centuries into ice, traps air as it falls to the ground. The trapped air contains oxygen and other gases. It also contains contaminants left behind by nature and human activity—contaminants such as sulfur from volcanic eruptions, cosmic debris from periodic disturbances on the sun, pesticide residues, and carbon dioxide from the burning of coal, oil, gas, and wood.

Scientists can learn a great deal about the climate of the past by analyzing the various gases and contaminants found in the air. To do this, they drill cores from the glacial ice and then study the contents of the air trapped in the ice. In the 1980s, researchers did exactly that. They analyzed an ice core drilled by Soviet scientists in Antarctica. Their analysis revealed that temperature and carbon dioxide levels rose and fell at the same time over a period of 160,000 years. This finding strengthened the suspicion that world temperatures could be altered by the amount of carbon dioxide in the atmosphere.

In the recent past, during the last 100 to 150 years, greenhouse gases—especially carbon dioxide—have been rising again. One of the biggest reasons for this rise is the burning of fossil fuels.

Fossil fuels

Coal, oil, and natural gas are called fossil fuels because they are the remains of plants and animals that died hundreds of millions of years ago. When burned, fossil fuels are a powerful source of energy. They are abundant. They burn hotter and longer than other commonly used fuels such as trees, grass, and animal dung. The carbon in fossil fuels combines with oxygen in the air to produce carbon dioxide.

If only a few people burned a little coal or oil, carbon dioxide from fossil fuels would probably have little effect on the earth's atmospheric greenhouse. But about 5.3 billion people exist on the earth today. They burn hundreds of millions

Coal-burning power plants release huge amounts of carbon dioxide into the air.

of tons of fossil fuels every year. This adds 5.5 billion tons of carbon dioxide to the atmosphere every year. Two major culprits produce much of the carbon dioxide from fossil fuels: coal-burning power plants and gasoline-burning cars.

Power plants and automobiles

Until the 1930s, most power plants used water power to drive electric generators. But the demand for electricity overwhelmed the hydropower plants. Today, only 9.5 percent of electric power in the United States comes from water. Most electricity is generated by steam-driven turbines. Some power plants convert water into steam with nuclear power. However, 73 percent of the electric power plants in the United States burn fossil fuels, usually coal, to power their generators.

As the standard of living rises around the world and as consumers demand more electricity, fossil fuel use also grows. In the United States, energy use doubled between 1960 and 1989. Of the 472 million tons of coal used in the United States in 1965, just over half, or 244.8 million tons, was burned by utility companies. In 1989, 889.6 million tons of coal were used in the United States; 765.6 tons—more than three quarters—went to utility companies. That coal, which is mostly carbon, produces millions of tons of carbon dioxide.

The number of automobiles used for transportation, too, is growing. And that has also added to the amount of carbon dioxide in the atmosphere. Between 1900 and 1920, the use of gasoline in the United States went from four thousand gallons a year to four million gallons a year. Today there are 113 million automobiles on the road in the United States alone. That is almost one car for every two people. The United States

consumes 6,324 million barrels of oil a year (a barrel is equal to forty-two gallons). That is more than Japan, Germany, Italy, France, Canada, and Great Britain combined. Almost 63 percent of that oil goes into the fuel tanks of cars, buses, trucks, aircraft, and trains.

Cars and trucks contribute heavily to the carbon dioxide in the air. For every gallon of gas they use, cars emit 5.6 pounds of carbon into the air. The average car uses about 525 gallons of gas a year. That means that every car on the road puts roughly its own weight in carbon into the air every year.

The threat of global warming

Worldwide, fossil fuel use puts 5.5 billion tons of carbon dioxide into the air each year. That is about one ton of carbon for every person in the world. The earth provides natural cleaners that try to maintain the balance of carbon dioxide in the atmosphere. Plants remove about 3 percent of the carbon dioxide produced each year by both natural processes (such as plant decay) and the ac-

Nineteenth-century Swedish chemist Svante Arrhenius foresaw the potentially harmful effects of carbon dioxide emissions.

tions of human beings. Scientists have long believed that the ocean absorbs about 25 to 45 percent of the gas.

That still leaves more than half of the excess carbon dioxide produced by humans in the air. That extra two to three billion tons of carbon dioxide is beginning to add up.

As early as 1896, Swedish chemist Svante Arrhenius was concerned about the use of coal and the production of carbon dioxide. He estimated that if the amount of carbon dioxide in the air in the early 1800s doubled, the average global temperature would go up by 7°F to 10°F.

But the earth is huge, and the atmosphere is four to eleven miles thick. Can humans really change the balance of gases in the air? Some evidence suggests they already have. In Arrhenius's time, the level of carbon dioxide in the atmosphere was 280 parts per million (ppm). In 1958, when Charles Keeling of Scripps Institution of Oceanography measured the amount of carbon dioxide in the air on the 11,000-foot summit of the Mauna Loa volcano in Hawaii, carbon dioxide measured 315 ppm. Levels were recorded at 350 ppm by 1990, and the level keeps rising by 1.5 ppm per year.

Growing levels of carbon dioxide emissions

That does not sound like a lot of carbon dioxide, certainly not enough to worry about. But it only takes a little bit of carbon dioxide to keep the earth at a comfortable temperature. Arrhenius predicted that a carbon dioxide level of 560 ppm would raise the average world temperature as much as 10°F. Some scientists are convinced that the increase in carbon dioxide from 280 ppm in Arrhenius's time to 350 ppm today has already raised the average global temperature by 1°F.

And carbon dioxide emissions are climbing. In

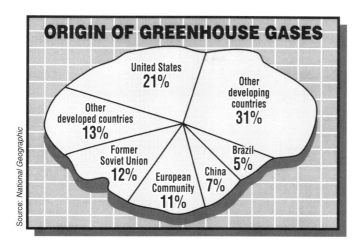

ORIGIN OF GREENHOUSE GASES

United States 21%

Other developing countries 31%

Other developed countries 13%

Former Soviet Union 12%

European Community 11%

China 7%

Brazil 5%

Source: National Geographic

most of the world, fossil fuel use is growing by 2 to 3 percent a year. In the United States, which gets 90 percent of its energy from fossil fuels, carbon dioxide emissions increased 31 percent between 1970 and 1985. Because of their high demand for energy, Americans produce ten times more carbon dioxide per person than the Chinese, who have lower energy demands.

China, however, plans to double its use of coal. In China, which has one quarter of the world's coal reserves and 1.1 billion people, coal use is growing by 5 percent a year. It is estimated that today, Chinese coal use contributes 10 percent of the carbon dioxide going into the world's atmosphere. By 2030, when its population is expected to reach 1.5 billion, China could be producing 20 percent of the world's carbon dioxide.

As the standard of living rises around the world, the demand for coal for electricity and oil for cars will also rise. As a result, there will be more carbon dioxide emissions. As if this were not enough, fossil fuel use is not the only way humans may be bringing about an endless summer.

2

Making Matters Worse

FOSSIL FUEL USE is not the only way humans may be altering the composition of the atmosphere and increasing the greenhouse effect. From industry to agriculture, daily practices produce carbon dioxide or other greenhouse gases that contribute to global warming. The burning of the rainforests is doubly destructive because it adds massive amounts of carbon dioxide to the air and because it removes the earth's natural air scrubbers: trees. Trees and other plants take billions of tons of carbon out of the air every year. They store the carbon in the tissues of their leaves, fruit, flowers, and bark. When plants die and decay, the carbon in them slowly combines with oxygen in the air and returns to the atmosphere as carbon dioxide. When trees are burned, however, the process takes hours instead of years. The carbon contained in the trees is immediately released into the atmosphere as carbon dioxide. Massive fires produce massive amounts of carbon dioxide. In 1988 alone, rainforest fires put 2.5 to 3 billion tons of carbon dioxide into the air. This adds to the greenhouse effect.

If there were fires in the rainforest only every five or ten years, the carbon dioxide these fires

(Opposite page) Barren patches of land reveal where slash-and-burn techniques cleared trees for farming in the Guatemalan rainforest.

25

produce would probably have little effect on global warming. But every year 55,000 square miles of rainforest are cut down and burned. That is an area the size of Illinois or New York. Of the 8 million square miles of tropical rainforest that once existed around the world, only 3.4 million square miles still stands. Most of it has disappeared in the last forty years. Some experts predict that the Amazonian rainforest in Brazil will be gone in another fifty years.

Although scientists and government officials are beginning to understand the scientific value and environmental importance of the rainforest, the trees continue to fall. The reason for this is usually economics. Many people in rainforest countries in South America, Africa, and South-

east Asia are poor. Most are crowded into urban areas without enough work, food, or housing. To ease the strain, many governments of rainforest countries encourage people to settle in and farm the rainforests. Thousands of people looking for a better life have done this.

The quickest, cheapest way to clear the land for farming is to cut down the trees and burn them, a technique often called slash and burn. However, this releases billions of tons of the greenhouse gases—carbon dioxide, methane, and nitrous oxide—into the atmosphere.

Although farmers have high expectations for their land, they are soon disappointed. Rainforest soil looks fertile, but it is really nutritionally poor. The enormous, fast-growing plants use up almost all the nutrients from fallen leaves, fruit, and flowers. Very little is left in the soil. So even though farmers may have a good crop for a year or two, soon the soil wears out and crops fail. The farmer moves on, burns another section of rainforest, and starts again. In the process, more greenhouse gases enter the atmosphere.

Clearing the land

Rainforest is also cleared and burned to provide grassland on which to raise cattle. But because the soil is poor, so is the quality of the grass. The cattle get little nutrition from eating it. They must eat much more of the nutritionally depleted grass to get the same nourishment they would get on richer grass. So, more rainforest land must be cleared to create more grassland to feed the cattle. The price is billions of tons of carbon dioxide entering the atmosphere and the loss of the rainforest trees that could remove it.

Logging practices in the tropical rainforests and in the moist, temperate forests of the Pacific Northwest in the United States and Canada add to

An Ivory Coast rainforest in Africa bears the scars of slash-and-burn tree clearing.

Many human activities including deforestation, release carbon dioxide and other pollutants into the atmsophere (A). Sunlight (B) penetrates the atmosphere to warm the earth. The earth's heat is trapped by carbon dioxide in the atmosphere (C), causing global warming.

the problem. Logging provides timber for houses and furniture and pulp for paper and synthetic fabrics. But when trees are cut for market, other trees are often damaged and left to die. As they decay, these trees release carbon into the air. In addition, the practice of clear-cutting, or removing all the trees in a given area, leaves no trees behind to reseed the forest floor. So there are fewer trees to clean carbon dioxide from the air.

Some scientists believe that environmentally unsound logging practices may be adding to the greenhouse effect in another way as well. The rotting material left on the forest floor is a rich feeding ground for termites, which produce another greenhouse gas during their digestive process: methane.

Methane traps heat

Methane is an odorless, colorless gas found in the atmosphere in traces of less than 2 parts per million (ppm). Like carbon dioxide, methane is a natural product. It is produced by anaerobic bacteria, microorganisms that live without oxygen. These microorganisms are found in the mud at the bottoms of swamps, marshes, ponds, lakes, and rivers. They also thrive in the intestinal tracts of animals and insects, such as termites.

Methane is twenty to thirty times more effective at trapping heat than carbon dioxide is. So even in small amounts, methane can make a big difference. In fact, methane accounts for 30 to 40 percent of the greenhouse effect today. And the level of methane gas in the atmosphere is rising.

In 1984, scientists took core samples from glaciers in Greenland and the Antarctic. The samples showed that until about three hundred to four hundred years ago, atmospheric methane levels had been constant at about .7 ppm. But then the levels began to climb. In the late 1960s, the methane level was at 1.4 ppm. Today it is 1.7 ppm and increasing by 1 to 2 percent a year. That means the amount in the atmosphere could more than double by 2050.

Where is all this methane coming from? Some of it seeps out of coal mines and oil wells. Natural gas, a fossil fuel, consists mostly of methane.

Cattle and other livestock can produce as much as 80 to 100 million tons of heat-trapping methane a year.

So, when natural gas pipelines and wells leak, they release methane into the air. Scientists disagree on where most of the methane in the air comes from. Rice fields, cattle, termites, and the frozen underground and undersea expanses of the Arctic are frequently mentioned. Some scientists think that as much as 70 percent of the methane in the air comes from these sources.

Rice, cattle, and termites

Much of the world's population subsists on a diet of rice. And as the population increases, so does the number of rice fields needed to feed those people. Costa Rica, for example, was once 20 percent tropical forest. Today, only 2 percent of the forest remains. Most of the rest of the land has been converted into rice fields.

In the still, muddy water of a rice field, anaerobic bacteria have abundant dead plant matter to feed on and much oxygenless mud to live in. In this environment they produce a great deal of methane gas—possibly 100 million tons a year.

The dark, moist, oxygenless intestinal tracts of animals also suit anaerobic microorganisms. Without these organisms, plant-eating animals (including humans) could not digest tough food fibers found in wood, leaves, vegetables, fruits, and grass. But as the bacteria break down the food, methane builds up, and the animal releases it as gas. Cattle and other livestock can produce as much as 80 to 100 million tons of methane a year.

Termites also produce methane. Estimates of how much vary but generally range from 25 million to 200 million tons annually. Termites create methane as they feed on dead wood, which is naturally abundant in the rainforest. But today, logging and burning leave surplus tons of woody material on the ground. All this dead wood is a feast for the termites. As a result, their numbers

Rice fields are feeding grounds for anaerobic bacteria which release tons of methane into the atmosphere.

are exploding, and so is the amount of methane they produce.

Some scientists are skeptical that the increasing amounts of atmospheric methane are from cattle, termites, and rice fields. Biologist George Woodwell of Woods Hole Oceanographic Institute in Massachusetts is one of these scientists. He believes the main source of excess methane in the atmosphere lies in the Arctic Circle.

Beneath the treeless regions of the Arctic under the permanently frozen soil called permafrost, methane and water combine to form compounds called methane hydrates. Methane hydrates are also found in the mud under the Arctic Ocean and at the bottom of deep sea trenches. For now, and probably for the foreseeable future, most methane hydrates are safely frozen under the permafrost and held tightly in place in the ocean by low temperatures and high pressures.

If the earth continues to warm, however, the permafrost could begin to thaw. The temperature of the oceans would rise. And the trapped methane could be released—perhaps as much as 600 million tons a year. In fact, scientists, including Woodwell, speculate that the 1°F increase in world temperatures over the past one hundred years may already be triggering a release of methane from the permafrost and the oceans.

A warming world could cause the permafrost of the Arctic Circle to melt, releasing methane into the air.

Positive feedback

This concerns scientists because methane may trigger what is called positive feedback. Positive feedback occurs when one event triggers a second, which then intensifies the first. Global warming, for example, releases methane from the permafrost, which makes the earth warmer, which triggers the release of more methane, and so on. Some scientists hypothesize that a positive methane feedback may have contributed to the ending of the last ice age eleven thousand years ago. As the ice melted, the water settled into depressions in the ground forming bogs, ponds, and lakes. In them, anaerobic bacteria started making methane. More methane raised temperatures, thawed more ice, and created more pools of standing water.

Such geophysical processes do not happen overnight. If they occur at all, geophysicist Gordon MacDonald believes, it may take five hundred to one thousand years for rising temperatures to release enough buried methane to cause the kind of change that occurred at the end of the last ice age.

Because methane traps heat so much more effectively than carbon dioxide does, even small increases in the atmosphere concern some scientists. These scientists also express concern about the increasing presence of nitrous oxide, a greenhouse gas that is two hundred times more effective at trapping heat than carbon dioxide is.

Nitrous oxide

Nitrous oxide is produced naturally and artificially. The atmosphere is 78 percent nitrogen and, although plants need nitrogen for food, they cannot use it directly from the air. It must first be converted by soil bacteria into ammonium then into nitrates before plants can absorb it. In the process, the bacteria release nitrous oxide gas.

Farmers often assist this natural process by adding chemical fertilizers containing nitrogen to the soil. The nitrogen appears in the form of ammonium nitrate, which when broken down in the soil by bacteria, releases nitrous oxide.

Nitrous oxide forms in other ways, too. Combustion produces nitrous oxide. When anything burns—whether it is a tree in the rainforest, natural gas in a stove, coal in a power plant, or gaso-

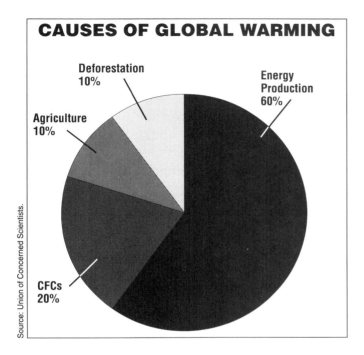

CAUSES OF GLOBAL WARMING

Deforestation
10%

Energy
Production
60%

Agriculture
10%

CFCs
20%

line in a car engine—nitrogen combines with oxygen to create nitrous oxide.

Scientists estimate that nitrous oxide levels in the atmosphere have increased 10 percent in the last one hundred years. Levels are rising, they add, by 0.3 percent or five million tons a year.

Over the last two decades, scientists have kept a close watch on at least one other contributor to the greenhouse effect. This contributor is known as chlorofluorocarbons, or CFCs.

CFCs

Chemist Thomas Midgley developed this miraculous group of chemicals in the 1930s. Chlorofluorocarbons were nontoxic and nonexplosive. Although first developed as a coolant for air conditioners and refrigerators, researchers soon found that CFCs had an astonishing variety of industrial applications. Since their invention, they have been used to blow foam for pillows, egg cartons, coffee cups, and fast-food packaging. They are used for insulation around pipes and inside trucks, as solvents to clean computer chips, as fumigants for granaries and cargo holds, and as the propellants in aerosol cans.

However, in the last twenty years, scientists have also discovered that CFCs can increase the greenhouse effect. First, CFCs are a far more effective greenhouse gas than carbon dioxide. One molecule of a chlorofluorocarbon can trap as much heat as ten thousand molecules of carbon dioxide. That makes them much more effective than carbon dioxide as greenhouse gases. But CFCs can influence the greenhouse effect in other ways as well.

CFCs are virtually indestructible. They are not destroyed or dissolved by any of the natural processes that normally cleanse the air. In fact, they may stay in the lower atmosphere for 100 to 120 years. Eventually, they rise into the stratosphere, or upper atmosphere. There they attack the ozone layer.

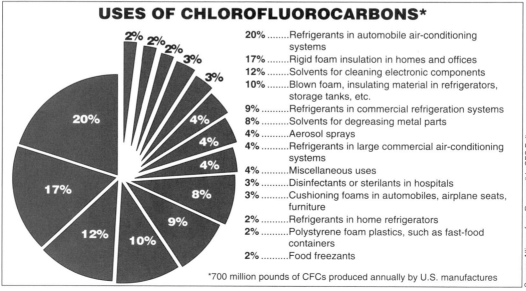

USES OF CHLOROFLUOROCARBONS*

20% ....Refrigerants in automobile air-conditioning systems
17% ....Rigid foam insulation in homes and offices
12% ....Solvents for cleaning electronic components
10% ....Blown foam, insulating material in refrigerators, storage tanks, etc.
9% ....Refrigerants in commercial refrigeration systems
8% ....Solvents for degreasing metal parts
4% ....Aerosol sprays
4% ....Refrigerants in large commercial air-conditioning systems
4% ....Miscellaneous uses
3% ....Disinfectants or sterilants in hospitals
3% ....Cushioning foams in automobiles, airplane seats, furniture
2% ....Refrigerants in home refrigerators
2% ....Polystyrene foam plastics, such as fast-food containers
2% ....Food freezants

*700 million pounds of CFCs produced annually by U.S. manufactures

Source: Alliance for a Responsible CFC Policy.

The ozone layer is a thin section of the earth's upper atmosphere composed of ozone, a gas made up of oxygen. The ozone layer filters out dangerous ultraviolet radiation from the sun and protects life on earth.

When CFCs rise into the stratosphere and come in contact with ultraviolet radiation, they break down the ozone into oxygen. As this breakdown occurs, the ozone layer weakens and thins. With enough thinning, the ozone layer can develop holes. These holes, and even some thin spots, allow potentially harmful amounts of ultraviolet radiation to reach the earth.

Too much ultraviolet radiation threatens all living things, but the link between this problem and the greenhouse effect lies with tiny ocean plants called phytoplankton. Phytoplankton remove millions of tons of carbon dioxide from the air every year. They do this through photosynthesis, the process plants use to store the sun's energy. This process helps keep the greenhouse effect in balance. But higher levels of ultraviolet radiation leaking through the atmosphere could kill the

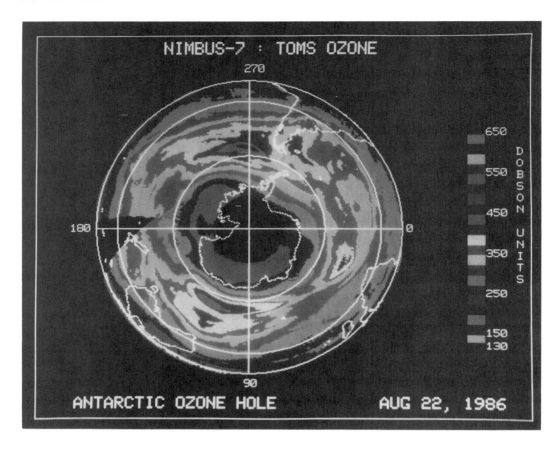

Scientists use computer-generated models of the Antarctic polar region to monitor changes in the ozone hole.

heavy concentrations of phytoplankton that live in the oceans. Without the minute ocean-dwelling plants to remove carbon dioxide from the air, the level of carbon dioxide in the atmosphere could rise quickly.

Scientists have found at least one ozone hole over the Antarctic and have identified thin spots over the Arctic and around the Northern Hemisphere. The ultraviolet radiation reaching the surface of the earth through holes and thin spots threaten to increase the greenhouse effect, Harvard scientist Michael McElroy says.

In 1989, eighty nations agreed to phase out CFC production by the year 2000. However, as University of California, Irvine, researcher

F. Sherwood Rowland pointed out in 1974, with a lifetime of 120 years, the molecules will be around a long time. "Ninety percent of the molecules now in the atmosphere will still be there by 2000 A.D., 39 percent by 2100 A.D., 17 percent by 2200 A.D., and 2 percent by 2300 A.D.," wrote Rowland. Even if humans stopped producing CFCs immediately, he added, they "will survive in the atmosphere for the next several centuries."

Although CFCs are no longer used in some products, they are still commonly found in appliances and in industry. Because of that, the level of CFCs in the atmosphere may go up another 10 to 20 percent before it levels off. Some scientists speculate that at those levels, the earth may lose 10 to 25 percent of its ozone by 2050. That is bound to influence the greenhouse effect and, as a result, global warming.

Some CFC manufacturers have already begun to make new versions that will have a shorter life and less effect on the ozone layer. However, some researchers think these second generation CFCs may actually be twice as effective as the old CFCs at trapping heat in the atmosphere.

Of the greenhouse gases in the atmosphere today, carbon dioxide makes up 60 percent; methane, 20 percent; CFCs, 15 percent; and nitrous oxide, 5 percent. Despite their smaller concentrations, the combined effect of methane, CFCs, and nitrous oxide may prove to be as harmful and maybe even more so than carbon dioxide alone.

Carbon dioxide, methane, nitrous oxide, and the chlorofluorocarbons all contribute to the greenhouse effect, and, in theory, could cause significant increases in temperatures on earth. But will they? Not everyone is convinced.

3

Does a Threat Really Exist?

IN 1988, JAMES Hansen of the National Aeronautics and Space Administration (NASA) Goddard Institute for Space Studies testified before the Senate Committee on Energy and Natural Resources. He told the committee he was 99 percent certain the 1°F rise in world temperatures since the 1850s had been caused by an increasing greenhouse effect. "It's time to stop waffling so much and say that the evidence is pretty strong that the greenhouse effect is here," he said.

Like Hansen, most scientists believe higher levels of greenhouse gases are causing global warming. But others say there is room for doubt. They argue that the earth has natural control mechanisms—called negative feedback—that keep the earth's climate in balance. Just as positive feedback intensifies a condition, negative feedback cancels one. Thus, higher temperatures due to an increasing greenhouse effect may naturally trigger events that will cool the earth and hold the climate in balance.

Some researchers believe the slight warming of the earth over the last 100 to 150 years is part of a long-term, natural cycle that has little to do with the production of greenhouse gases. A few voices

(Opposite page) A thick cloud of ash and steam spews from the Mount Pinatubo volcano. Scientists are still uncertain whether volcanic dust is one of nature's ways to counteract the greenhouse effect.

even warn that what humans have to fear is a cooling world, not a warming one.

Although the atmosphere plays a leading role in controlling the earth's climate, the planet's ability to reflect light also controls climate. The earth's natural reflective ability is called albedo. Many think the earth's albedo can counteract the global warming trend.

Albedo can be seen at work in desert regions where people often wear white clothes because white reflects light and heat and keeps them cooler. Dark colors, particularly black, absorb light and heat.

What works for people on a small scale gener-

Thunderclouds above the Amazon Basin in Brazil. Low, dense, water-filled clouds cool the atmosphere by reflecting sunlight into space.

ally works for the earth on a global scale. White or light-colored areas, such as clouds, ice, and snow, reflect sunlight back into space, cooling the earth below. Dark surfaces have the opposite effect. Exposed rock and soil absorb heat and warm the earth.

The role of clouds

Because clouds have the potential to cool the earth, some researchers see them as an effective means of controlling a rise in global temperatures. They say that as the earth warms, more water will evaporate and condense into clouds. More clouds will reflect sunlight into space, keeping the earth cool. Unfortunately, not all clouds reflect sunlight back into space. Some actually transmit the sun's radiation to the earth and trap it there.

Low, dense, water-filled clouds, which contain millions of tiny droplets, provide millions of surfaces from which sunlight can reflect back into space. These clouds could be important in reducing the greenhouse effect, perhaps cutting a potential two-degree temperature rise in half. "A few tenths of a percentage point change in the number of droplets per cloud can totally reverse the greenhouse effect," atmospheric scientist Robert Charlson says.

High, thin, icy clouds, though, heat things up. Unlike low, dense clouds, high, thin ones transmit the sun's radiation to earth. They then trap the heat radiated by the planet, much like a greenhouse gas. So some researchers believe high, thin clouds could double any temperature rise due to an increasing greenhouse effect.

To find out exactly how clouds will affect global warming—whether they will warm or cool a greenhouse world—atmospheric scientist Veerabhadran Ramanathan and his colleagues at

Scripps Institution of Oceanography in San Diego, California, are studying clouds and cloud formation. The information they gather helps give them a truer picture of what global temperatures in the future might be if greenhouse gas levels continue to rise.

"Clouds are one of the most poorly understood phenomena in earth science," Ramanathan told a San Diego newspaper in 1991. "The uncertain role of clouds is one of the primary reasons for our inability to make accurate predictions about global warming."

Cooling dust

Clouds are not the only elements in the atmosphere that can cool a warming planet. Dust particles in the upper atmosphere also reflect sunlight

away from the earth. Most of this dust comes from volcanic eruptions. Although some scientists believe volcanic ash may reduce global warming only temporarily, others say it may be one of nature's long-term methods for cooling the earth.

Volcanic eruptions can dramatically affect the earth's climate. In 1815, for example, the volcano Tambora erupted in Indonesia. Millions of tons of ash were thrown high into the stratosphere. There, it floated around the world, blocking out sunlight and wreaking havoc with global climates. Temperatures on earth dropped by almost 2°F. The following year, 1816, was called "the year without a summer" in the Northern Hemisphere. In New England, where summers are usually hot and sticky, snow fell in June, and frost covered the ground all summer. In Europe and India, crops failed due to severe weather.

Mount Pinatubo

The year 1991 gave scientists a fresh opportunity to study the effects of volcanic dust on the earth's climate. On June 12 and 13, Mount Pinatubo erupted in the Philippines. It sent an estimated twenty to thirty million tons of dust and sulfur dioxide particles into the stratosphere. "In terms of atmospheric effects, Pinatubo was probably the biggest thing in the century," according to volcanologist Robert Tilling at the U.S. Geological Survey.

Within three months, the dust cloud had spread around the world. Scientific instruments detected a change in weather almost immediately. In the Caribbean, scientists measured a 33 percent reduction in the amount of sunlight reaching the earth. Weather satellites used by the National Oceanic and Atmospheric Administration (NOAA) showed a four-degree temperature drop in the tropics.

Billowing smoke, dust, and ash fill the air around the erupting Mount Pinatubo volcano. Temperatures worldwide began to drop as the volcano's dust cloud spread through the atmosphere.

Worldwide, as the volcanic cloud spreads out, average temperatures could cool by as much as 1°F. Although some argue that the Pinatubo eruption will reduce the greenhouse effect, the cooling will probably only be temporary. Once the dust settles, the earth could be back in a warming greenhouse.

Scientists are still trying to determine whether volcanic dust really is one of nature's tools for counteracting the greenhouse effect. If it is, nature may have many other similar tools. The largest and possibly the most mysterious of these tools may be the world's oceans.

The power of the oceans

The oceans act as a natural air scrubber by absorbing excess carbon dioxide from the atmosphere. Carbon dioxide passes into the oceans by combining with seawater and through absorption by phytoplankton. The carbon dioxide is stored in the oceans usually in the deepest, coldest regions.

Various researchers have claimed the ocean is capable of absorbing anywhere between 20 percent to 70 percent of the excess carbon dioxide in the air. That amounts to at least 2 to 3 billion tons of the approximately 8.5 billion tons of carbon dioxide added to the atmosphere each year by human activities.

Scientists have even thought that the increasing levels of carbon dioxide in the air might trigger the oceans to absorb more carbon dioxide. This is because when a liquid and gas are in contact with each other, the amount of gas the liquid can dissolve increases as the amount of gas in the air increases. Simply put, the more carbon dioxide in the air, the more could be dissolved in the oceans. As a result, researchers thought that the oceans would go a long way toward reducing the risk of global warming through an increased greenhouse effect.

But in 1957, Roger Revelle and Hans E. Suess of Scripps Institution of Oceanography gave the first warning that the oceans might not be absorbing as much carbon dioxide as expected. Their findings appear to be confirmed in a recent study by a team of scientists from NOAA, NASA, and the Lamont-Doherty Geological Survey. The study indicates that the oceans may absorb only one billion tons of carbon dioxide a year. That sounds like a lot, but it actually only accounts for a small part of the excess carbon dioxide.

Oceans store less carbon dioxide than scientists once thought, and they store it only temporarily. Some of it eventually comes back to the surface when the deep currents, moving toward the equator, warm and rise. Some researchers have claimed that this carbon dioxide-rich water stimulates the growth of phytoplankton, which absorb more carbon dioxide from the air. However, according to the joint NOAA, NASA, Lamont-Doherty study, as temperatures of the earth, air, and ocean increase, water rich in carbon dioxide may actually release the gas into the air rather than absorb it.

This is because warm water holds less carbon dioxide than cold water holds. So as cold water heats up, the carbon dioxide must be released into the atmosphere. As a result, warming oceans could actually increase the greenhouse effect, not counteract it. The result could be significant. The oceans contain sixty times more carbon dioxide than the atmosphere. If the oceans warmed enough to release only 5 percent of the carbon dioxide stored in deep, cold water, the amount of carbon dioxide in the atmosphere could go up by 25 percent.

A long process

The new study also points out that it takes the oceans one hundred to one thousand years to cycle carbon dioxide out of the atmosphere. So the oceans are probably not a short-term answer to reducing global temperatures.

However, the oceans are not an immediate threat to climate stability, either. It takes a long time to raise the temperature of so vast a body of water. It also takes continually increasing temperatures. And there are a few scientists who say the

warming trend that has been noticed in the last one hundred years may not continue indefinitely. That is because they believe the warming they have seen is due less to an increasing greenhouse effect and more to normal, natural sunspot cycles.

Oceans absorb excess carbon dioxide. Some researchers warn that oceans could actually increase the greenhouse effect by releasing carbon dioxide into the atmosphere.

Warming through sunspots

Sunspots are dark spots on the face of the sun. They result from magnetic storms on the sun's surface. During times of intense sunspot activity, the sun gets brighter and throws off more radiation. More radiation could cause the earth to heat up. So some researchers believe changes in the earth's climate—those occurring now and those that occurred in the past—may be linked to sunspot activity.

Sunspot activity occurs in overlapping cycles. The length of the cycles varies. Scientists have

Some scientists believe peak periods of sunspot activity may explain higher temperatures over the past one hundred years.

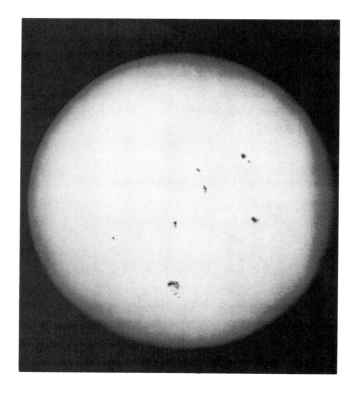

identified eleven-year, seventy-year, and two-hundred-year cycles in which sunspot activity rises to a peak and then falls. Scientists studying this phenomenon have noticed that temperatures rise when peak periods coincide. They have also noted falling temperatures during low periods of sunspot activity.

Between 1650 and 1710, during a period called the "little ice age" in Europe, winters were unusually cold, and spring and summer growing seasons were very short. Researcher Jack Eddy analyzed historical records from this time and found that the exceptionally cold temperatures coincided with a low period in sunspot activity.

During the 1980s, scientists noticed that two cycles of solar activity appeared to be building to a peak. Astrophysicist Sallie Baliunas and others believe the overlapping peak sunspot activity may have contributed to the higher temperatures of the last one hundred years.

If, as some researchers suggest, sunspot activity actually does affect the earth's temperature, then it is likely that temperatures will continue to periodically rise and fall. This would, in essence, create a natural balance in the greenhouse effect.

Despite these and other arguments, most scientists believe the earth may be in for some warm times ahead. Naturally, concerned citizens and government officials want to know what this will mean to their way of life. There are no crystal balls of climate prediction, however. So scientists must rely on a variety of tools, techniques, and their own skills and intuition to chart the future.

4

Living in a Hothouse

THERE IS NO way of knowing for certain how warm the future might be and what a warmer world might be like. Yet the questions of how hot it will get and how that will affect life on earth are at the heart of the greenhouse effect controversy. This is because some scientists predict massive climate changes if temperatures on earth rise by the maximum 10°F predicted. An increase of this magnitude, some scientists suspect, would completely reverse world climates. Farmlands could become deserts; deserts could turn into lush gardens.

Not all scientists go along with this view. Some predict the earth's climates will change very little or will stay the same. A few think it might even get cooler. "When you first look into climate change, you realize how little you know," says Ralph Cicerone, atmospheric chemist at the University of California, Irvine. "The more you look into it, the more you realize how little anyone knows."

For the most part, scientists base their predictions of the future on computer models. In a sense, these models are the scientists' crystal balls.

A model, such as a model car, model plane, or

(Opposite page) Some researchers warn that a substantial increase in the greenhouse effect could reverse world climates, causing fertile farmlands to become hot and dry.

globe of the earth, represents something in the real world. Models, even realistic ones such as radio-controlled cars, are not identical to the objects they represent. But they do tell something about that object.

Unlike physical models that represent objects, computer models can represent natural systems, such as the world's environment. Scientists create computer models by describing natural processes through mathematical formulas. Scientists develop their formulas from facts, figures, and their own understanding of how the natural world works.

Calculating the future

Computer models also rely on assumptions. Scientists might assume that past rainfall patterns will remain the same in the future, for example. Or they might have reason to assume rainfall patterns will change. These assumptions, too, are included in the mathematical computer model.

Once the facts and assumptions have been built into the model, scientists begin to change the conditions in the model world. They alter the carbon dioxide level, temperatures, cloud patterns, and ocean currents, for example. The computer then shows them what physical changes might occur in the real world if those changes took place.

Because the facts, figures, and assumptions that make up a computer model vary, so do the results. This is why some scientists studying the greenhouse effect foresee a topsy-turvy world, while others predict little change at all.

Despite the differences most models agree on two basic points. First, if fossil fuel emissions are not reduced, atmospheric carbon dioxide will double by 2050. Second, the increase in carbon dioxide will cause the earth's average tempera-

ture to rise by 3°F to 10°F.

Scientists do not know for certain what this kind of temperature increase would mean. Using computer models along with historical, geological, and other records they can, however, develop theories.

Scientists know, for example, that the earth experienced six years of record high temperatures during the 1980s. These temperatures averaged only one to two degrees above normal. Nevertheless, during this period, rainfall slackened, and several regions of the world experienced severe drought.

Heat and drought on this scale can damage crops. The U.S. corn crop, for example, suffered serious damage in the 1980s. Crop yields were down by 35 percent, or 2.6 billion bushels. Heat

Scientists use computer models to calculate how continued fossil fuel emissions will affect the earth's atmosphere.

was one part of the problem, disease was another. In 1989, after the hot, dry summer of 1988, much of the U.S. corn harvest was found to be infected with a cancer-causing mold and had to be destroyed. Rice, too, is susceptible to damage from drought and high heat. So scientists theorize that global warming even at the low end of the temperature scale could damage many food crops that sustain human life around the world.

Theories about life in an even hotter world are much less certain since modern humans have never experienced a temperature rise as drastic as 10°F. A temperature change on that scale did occur in the earth's distant past, about ten thousand years ago. When that happened, whole environments changed, and the ice age came to an end.

Cold, wet regions, such as the area now known as the Los Angeles basin, turned warm and dry. Cold-weather mammals, such as the wooly mammoths, giant ground sloths, dire wolves, and saber-toothed cats that once roamed this area, died. Certain snails could not tolerate the temperature change either. They are now found only in

Cracked, dry earth in drought-stricken California. Severe drought could damage many food crops that are necessary for human survival.

cooler mountain climes. Giant redwood trees, once plentiful there, withered in the heat. Today, conditions and temperatures more hospitable to the trees are found about four hundred miles north.

This appears to have happened in other areas, too. Evidence of dramatic environmental change can be seen in the dry, mostly treeless Sahara Desert of North Africa. The Sahara, Harvard University botantist Rob Nicholson and others, believe, once was a grassy savannah, or plain, with enough rain to support cypress trees. A few of these trees still stand in what is now a dry streambed. Researchers suspect that most of the trees and grass died out when temperatures

A drastic temperature change about ten thousand years ago caused cold, wet regions to turn warm and dry. Cold-weather mammals such as the wooly mammoth died because they could not tolerate the temperature change.

changed and transformed the region from grassy plain to desert.

Temperature change can also cause cool regions to expand farther and farther north. Botanists estimate a temperature increase of less than 1.8°F could force a tree's preferred climate 60 to 100 miles north over ten years. Within sixty years, a tree's habitat could be as much as 120 to 400 miles north.

The trees' migration

Although people and animals might migrate quickly when climates change, trees relocate slowly. They must first disperse their seeds, which then turn into seedlings. The seedlings must grow to trees and in turn disperse their seeds. Tree species can move toward a suitable climate no faster than about one-half mile a year.

Because the trees' preferred climate would be moving north faster than the trees could follow it, at the very least, the composition of the forests would begin to change. At worst, they could die and disappear.

This does not mean that trees and forests would disappear overnight. Trees might die slowly, over years. The seedlings might continue to grow in less favorable climate, but they might be stunted or might not produce seeds at all. The forest itself might remain, but altered conditions might change the mix of trees.

As cold regions move farther north, they leave behind warmer temperatures. If this were to happen, areas that are now either covered with ice and snow or that have severe winters and short growing seasons might become good crop-growing regions. Scientists know this can happen because in the past, northern regions were farmed when the earth warmed. According to ancient records, olives and wine grapes, which demand

warm, dry weather, were grown in northern Italy. Vineyards also thrived in England, which is now noted for its damp, chilly climate. Oats and barley, both warm-weather crops, were harvested in Iceland, which is frozen now in the winter.

Farmers might find that their crops actually grow bigger in a world experiencing a heightened greenhouse effect. Because plants feed on carbon dioxide, higher levels would mean more food for plants. In laboratory tests under ideal conditions, plants grew bigger when they were exposed to more carbon dioxide. Bigger plants probably would require more fertilizer and more water. Depending on the region the crops are grown in, in a greenhouse world, that extra water might not be available.

This is because a warmer world could mean less rain and snow in certain areas. Runoff from rain and snow fills lakes, reservoirs, and rivers and seeps into the ground to be stored there. But a 3°F temperature increase in the western United States could reduce rain and snow by 10 percent in the Rockies, decreasing runoff and available water. In the basins of the Colorado and the Rio Grande rivers, runoff could decrease by 40 to 75 percent, affecting the amount of fresh water available for farming.

The oceans

A warming world due to an increased greenhouse effect will create changes not only on the land but also in the oceans. For a warmer atmosphere will also warm the oceans. Warming oceans could change weather around the world. One way warmer seas could alter the world's weather patterns is by changing the El Niño.

The El Niño is a meteorological, or weather, event that occurs every three to five years off the west coast of South America. It seems to coincide with changes in weather and rainfall patterns around the world. Scientists still do not know much about what triggers the El Niño condition. However, they do know that it occurs when the normally cool waters along the South American coast warm up, sending columns of warmed air into the atmosphere. This rising warm air may change the path of jet streams, high-altitude currents of air known to affect the weather. As a result, the El Niño in the southeastern Pacific causes droughts in Australia, Brazil, and Mozambique. It almost always causes the Indian monsoon to fail; rain falls over the ocean and not over the Indian subcontinent. The El Niño can also

cause storms along the west coast of North and South America.

Because the El Niño occurs when one part of the ocean warms, scientists worry that oceans warmed by an increased greenhouse effect could bring more frequent El Niño years. With them might come hotter, drier summers and drought.

The oceans already appear to be warming. Records of surface seawater temperatures kept since the 1800s indicate that ocean temperatures increased by approximately 1°F between 1920 and 1940 and have increased another one degree since 1970. This may have intensified the unusual El Niño pattern in the 1980s. Meteorologists suspect that two El Niño conditions back-to-back

An increase in global temperatures could greatly decrease runoff into the Colorado River. This would, in turn, reduce the amount of fresh water available for farming.

during that time were at least partially responsible for the severe drought suffered by the central United States. Five of the hottest summers recorded in the last 130 years were in the 1980s, with the hottest year being 1988. In 1986 (an El Niño year), Canadian winter temperatures rose on some days by as much as 15°F.

In addition to increased El Niño conditions, warming water could cause more frequent and more severe coastal storms. This would be especially true for hurricanes, which draw their strength from the heat rising from a warmer ocean. The warmer the ocean's surface water and the deeper that warm water runs, the more powerful the storm. Hurricanes could become 40 or 50 percent more severe if ocean temperatures increase by only a few degrees. This could be disastrous for coastal cities, resorts, harbors, and wetlands.

The high-water line

Hurricanes may not be the only threat to the coasts from a warming ocean. Coastlines may be in danger from rising sea level.

Sea level is not constant; it can change. For example, 100,000 years ago, the sea level was twenty feet higher than today. During the last ice age, with much of the water frozen in polar caps and glaciers, the sea was three hundred feet lower.

Because the level of the sea has appeared constant, however, human beings have built cities and harbors close to the water line. Many major world cities are less than fifty feet above sea level. These include: Boston, Massachusetts; Dhaka, Bangladesh; Galveston, Texas; Honolulu, Hawaii; Miami, Florida; New Orleans, Louisiana; Rio de Janeiro, Brazil; San Diego, California; San Francisco, California; Seattle, Washington;

Sydney, Australia; and Tokyo, Japan. Venice, Italy, sits in a series of canals right at sea level. Amsterdam in the Netherlands is actually below sea level. It is protected from the ocean by a series of dikes or sea walls. If ocean levels were to rise, these cities and the millions of people living in them would be endangered.

Rising temperatures are expected to push the level of the oceans higher in the future. One reason is that as water warms, it takes up more room. This is called thermal expansion, and some experts estimate it could raise sea level by one to five feet over the next fifty years as temperatures

Hurricanes, which draw strength from heat rising from water, could become more frequent and severe if the greenhouse effect substantially warms the oceans.

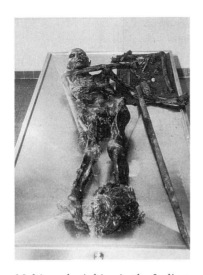

Melting glacial ice in the Italian Alps revealed the mummified body of a hunter who lived during the ice age.

climb. In the last one hundred years, sea level has risen by about five inches. Three to four inches of that rise is a result of thermal expansion.

Thermal expansion will not be the only cause of sea level rise, however. Global warming is expected to melt glaciers and polar ice. In fact, climatologists believe ice is melting now due to the 1°F increase in global temperatures in the last one hundred years. Since 1850, the Grindelwald Glacier in Switzerland has crept back about one mile. In 1991, the mummified body of an ice age hunter was found in the Italian Alps, half exposed by the melting of the ice. Melting glacial ice has contributed one to two inches to today's higher sea level. Enough water is contained in the world's glaciers to raise sea level by ten feet.

The polar caps, the ice-covered areas around the North and South poles, contain enough water to bring the oceans up by about 250 feet. The ice covering Antarctica is estimated to contain about as much water as the North Atlantic Ocean, most of it in East Antarctica. If the ice there melted, estimates James Titus, senior scientist with the U.S. Environmental Protection Agency (EPA), it could produce more than two hundred feet of rise in the ocean.

Antarctica

Although scientists believe that the ice in East Antarctica has melted to some extent during warm periods in the past, they do not believe it has completely melted at any time in the last two million years. It is considered stable for now.

The West Antarctica ice sheet is not as dependable. The ice field there could disintegrate within forty years, according to some estimates, although it would more likely take several centuries. It might also take a temperature increase between 12.6°F and 18°F to melt the ice, much more than most scientists foresee in the near future. But if the ice did melt, it could contribute another twenty-three feet to the sea level. In fact, about 100,000 years ago, during the last interglacial period, sea level was higher by just about this amount. Some scientists believe this may have been caused by water from the West Antarctic ice sheet, which may have melted at that time.

Currently sea level is rising by about one inch per decade. The EPA estimates that with continued greenhouse warming, the oceans could rise by as much as 4.7 feet to more than 7 feet by 2100. Although some estimates of future sea levels are higher and some are lower, most scientists think a temperature increase of 1.5°F will cause about a three-foot rise in the oceans. That may not seem like a lot, but on most gently sloping beaches, it would mean that the waves would reach almost three hundred feet above the current

Scientists believe that the ice in East Antarctica is in no immediate danger of melting, but that the ice sheet in West Antarctica is less stable.

tide line. In many areas, that would affect homes, businesses, hotels, and highways. The EPA estimates that three thousand to ten thousand acres of oceanfront land would be lost.

Rising sea levels would also inundate most river deltas in the world along with estuaries and many low-lying islands. Cities would be flooded, cropland destroyed, fishing grounds disturbed, and people displaced. Rising water would push salt water up rivers, poisoning drinking water in many areas.

Human survival

Contaminated drinking water, decreased food supply, and poorer quality food would certainly have an effect on human health. But if the carbon dioxide in the atmosphere were to double and raise global temperatures by the predicted 3°F to 10°F, it could have even more far-reaching effects.

Daily life for many people would probably be more uncomfortable. Most areas of the world will not only have hotter days, but also more of them. For example, according to the NASA Goddard Institute for Space Studies' computer model, Dallas, Texas, could have as many as seventy-eight days a year at temperatures higher than 100°F. Presently, Dallas averages nineteen days a year above 100°F. One hundred and sixty-two days of the year could exceed 90°F.

Although there have been few studies on the effect of rising temperatures on human health, one study done by the University of Delaware indicates that this kind of temperature rise could increase the number of heat-related deaths more than six times. Seventy percent of the deaths would occur among the elderly. But heat waves could also push up the numbers of premature births, miscarriages, and newborn deaths.

Other studies have shown that the number of cases of heart and lung disease increases when the temperature rises. Higher temperatures also are often accompanied by higher air pollution levels in cities. This could aggravate problems for people with lung conditions, such as asthma or emphysema.

Extreme heat not only causes pre-existing illnesses to worsen, it can indirectly cause other diseases as well. High temperatures often result in more insects. In a warmer world, diseases

Buildings are barely visible on this smoggy day in Los Angeles. Higher temperatures can cause higher levels of air pollution.

spread by insects might infect increasing numbers of people. Studies by ecologist Andrew Dobson, for example, have shown that tsetse flies, which carry sleeping sickness, would probably spread with an increase in temperatures. Some scientists have speculated that numbers of mosquitoes, too, might increase causing more illnesses, such as yellow and dengue fever.

Other risks to human beings are more difficult to calculate. The threat of war is one such risk. As the Smithsonian Institution's Thomas E. Lovejoy points out, "If you want to have political stability, you have to have environmental stability."

Lovejoy and others are looking at the potential for conflict in a warmer world. If drought and famine become widespread, if oceans rise to flood seaside cities, people will become refugees. As they move into other regions, conflict could occur. That conflict can "come about simply by [people] deserting their land and moving to a neighboring country," according to Kilaparti Ramakrishna, international environmental law expert at the Woods Hole Research Center in Massachusetts. But U.S. senator Albert Gore from Tennessee writes in his book *Earth in the Balance* that "international tensions [could worsen] to the point of actual warfare, including the risk of nuclear war."

The future at risk

Three hundred scientists and world leaders considered this view during a 1988 global warming conference in Canada. "Humanity is conducting an unintended, uncontrolled, globally pervasive experiment whose ultimate consequences could be second only to a global nuclear war," wrote H.L. Ferguson, conference director for that meeting. "The best predictions available indicate

U.S. senator Albert Gore believes that an unstable environment could lead to political instability worldwide.

potentially severe economic and social dislocation for the present and future generations, which will worsen international tensions and increase risk of conflicts between and within nations."

These predictions do not have to come true. Although most scientists believe there will be a 3°F to 4°F temperature increase in the future, they also believe that, if human beings take serious steps now, they can keep the world livable for all.

Turning the Tide of the Future

No matter what human beings do, the earth may warm by at least 1.5°F by 2030, thanks primarily to excess greenhouse gases in the atmosphere. However, many scientists think that if people act together—and quickly—they can keep the temperature from rising any higher. But what should be done? And who should do it?

Ideas for reducing the greenhouse effect are surprisingly numerous. Most of these ideas can be acted on now or in the near future. Many require small adjustments in daily living. A few depend on technological advances or changes in society.

The answer to the second question is simple: Everyone must be involved. Many people already are. Governments, businesses, and individuals must all participate in solving the problem. There can be no spectators. The decisions people make today might well change the world for future generations.

The quick fix

Researchers have proposed a number of quick fixes to hold back global warming, although even these researchers acknowledge some of these

(Opposite page) A solar thermal power plant in California. Replacing fossil fuels with solar energy could help reduce the greenhouse effect.

ideas are not practical. Thomas Stix of Princeton University, in Princeton, New Jersey, for example, has proposed destroying CFCs with beams from mountain-top lasers. Wallace Broecker, geochemist at Lamont-Doherty, has suggested spreading thirty-five million tons of sulfur dioxide in the stratosphere to reflect sunlight back into space. Biologist John Martin of Moss Landing Marine Labs in California has suggested seeding the ocean around Antarctica with iron. Phytoplankton in the water would feed on the iron, grow faster, and absorb more carbon dioxide in the process. Michael McElroy of Harvard University in Cambridge, Massachusetts, has proposed setting reflectors in space to direct sunlight to the Arctic and Antarctic oceans. In theory, this

Newly planted trees now appear on what was once a gravel pit. Reforestation is one way to slow global warming, some scientists believe.

would stimulate photosynthesis, which would cause phytoplankton to absorb more carbon dioxide. The mirrors could also cool the earth by deflecting sunlight into space.

Intriguing as these ideas are, most scientists agree that the solutions to limiting the greenhouse effect will be more down-to-earth. The only realistic way to slow global warming, says Rodney Fujita, staff scientist at the Environmental Defense Fund, is "cutting fossil fuel combustion, stopping deforestation, and reforesting degraded lands."

Technological quick fixes can also lead to false hope, says Senator Albert Gore. For these solutions allow people to think "there is no need for fundamental change in the design of our civilization and that, with a little creative engineering, we can outsmart nature once again. . . . The truth is that only by changing our behavior can we effectively address the global environmental problems we face."

Kicking the fossil fuel habit

That behavior can be changed in many ways, but the biggest step would be a reduction in greenhouse gases entering the atmosphere. Because fossil fuel burning contributes the greatest amount of greenhouse gases to the atmosphere, reducing fossil fuel use could reduce global warming. This reduction can be achieved in many ways.

One way is to increase use of solar energy and decrease use of coal for producing electricity. The sun's energy can be converted to electric power in several ways. The most promising of these is through the use of solar, or photovoltaic, cells. Today these cells can convert only about 6 percent of the sun's energy into electricity. However, by the year 2000, researchers expect to be able to

A photovoltaic power system. Solar panels are used to convert the sun's energy into electricity.

channel 12 to 20 percent of the sun's light into electricity through photovoltaics. One prototype photovoltaic cell converts 30 to 40 percent of the light striking it into usable electric power.

Other solar energy options are already in use. Luz International, Ltd., in the Mojave Desert, converts the sun's heat into power by using it to create steam from water. The steam runs an electric generator that provides electricity to homes and businesses in Southern California. Solar power is clean to use and limitless. It burns no fossil fuels and therefore produces no greenhouse gases. As a result, switching to solar technology for energy would reduce the greenhouse effect.

Although solar power is promising, a combination of solar energy and hydrogen-power technology could further reduce fossil fuel use. Solar energy would be used to split water into hydrogen and oxygen. Then the hydrogen—in gas, liquid, or solid form—could be used as a fuel to power electric plants and transportation, such as cars and airplanes. Because the solar/hydrogen plant would use no fossil fuels, it would produce no greenhouse gases. Using solid or liquid hydrogen fuel would not produce greenhouse gases, either, although burning hydrogen gas would produce some nitrous oxides.

Some predict that, with the necessary financing, a solar/hydrogen power plant could be built by the end of the century in the United States. In Germany, however, hydrogen technology is already being embraced. The BMW car company, Siemens electronics, a Bavarian utilities company, the Messerschmitt-Boelkow-Blohm aerospace company, Linde gas company, and the German government are building a photovoltaic/hydrogen plant to produce hydrogen gas. They will mix the hydrogen with natural gas and use it to fuel BMWs, city buses, and airplanes. They will also use the gas to power industrial machinery. The Germans are so confident in the future of hydrogen, they have already laid pipe in Dusseldorf to transport the gas to industry.

Changing the rules of the road

In addition to running on hydrogen gas, cars could also run on very efficient hydrogen fuel cells. Fuel cells convert 60 percent of the fuel into energy as opposed to only 40 percent in gasoline-driven cars. They create no greenhouse gases and no smog. They produce only water.

Electric cars, too, could replace gasoline-burning cars. Electric cars were widely used in the early part of the century. But they could only go about 50 to 80 miles before they had to be recharged. Recharging is still a problem, but BMW has developed a prototype sodium-sulfur battery that has a range of 125 miles and the pickup of a conventional subcompact car.

In the United States, General Motors, too, is developing an electric car prototype. The company was spurred into action by a decision of the California Air Resources Board. This board, which oversees state air quality standards, established new rules which require 2 percent of the new vehicles sold in California to be electric by 1998; by 2003, 10 percent must be electric. More than 200,000 cars are sold in California every year. So this represents a large market to car manufacturers. As a result, other carmakers are beginning to investigate the possibilities of electric cars.

Hydrogen and electric cars are not yet practical. Unlike gasoline-burning cars, hydrogen and electric cars cannot simply fuel up at the local gas station. These new-technology cars would need a

A man peers under the hood of an electric car which has a top speed of 100 miles per hour and a range of 125 miles between chargings.

place for replacing or recharging their batteries, and no such network of service stations exists.

Until a system of this sort is developed, people can reduce carbon dioxide emissions in other ways. They can use mass transportation, including buses and trains, to cut down on the number of cars on the road. Although most buses and trains currently burn gasoline and diesel fuel, countries including Germany and Japan are working on forms of mass transportation that do not burn fossil fuels or produce greenhouse gases. One of these is the maglev, a train propelled by powerful electromagnets. When it is put into use, it is expected to travel faster than three hundred miles per hour.

Greenhouse gases can also be reduced by driving cars that use fuel efficiently. Fuel or energy efficiency means using less fuel to get the same amount of energy. If all cars on the road got forty miles to the gallon, for example, oil use would decrease by 2.5 million barrels a day. That would

Germany's maglev train powered by electromagnets produces no greenhouse gases.

drastically reduce the amount of carbon dioxide released into the atmosphere.

Toyota has developed an energy-efficient prototype diesel engine that gets 110 miles to the gallon using one quarter of the fuel of a traditional car. Although it would not eliminate carbon dioxide emissions, this type of car would reduce them because it requires less fuel for greater distances.

Energy efficiency

People can become more energy efficient in their homes and businesses as well as in their cars. Household appliances, for example, waste a great deal of energy. More efficient use of energy would lower demand for electricity, which would reduce the need for coal to power the electric plants. Less coal burned would mean less carbon dioxide going into the atmosphere and a reduction in global warming.

Energy efficiency can start at the power plant itself through a process called cogeneration. Power plants produce tremendous amounts of heat. Usually that heat escapes into the air, where it dissipates and cannot be used. Cogenerating plants, however, recycle the heat and use it to create more steam to power the electric generators. So much power can be generated by the process that in the town of Vesterås, Sweden, the electricity used for all lighting and space heating comes from cogeneration. By using the trapped heat instead of releasing it, power plants use less coal to produce the same amount of energy and so produce fewer greenhouse gases.

Individual households can also play a part in reducing the greenhouse effect. Insulation keeps the temperature in a house constant, reducing the demands on the heating and cooling systems. Energy efficient appliances also reduce energy use.

Tons of Carbon Dioxide Emitted During A Car's Lifetime

57.75 Tons

37.71 Tons

25.93 Tons

Source: Energy Conservation Coalition.

18.0   27.5   45.0

FUEL EFFICIENCY
(miles per gallon)

For example, a refrigerator produced by Sun-Frost, a small company in California, cuts energy cost by 85 percent. An energy-efficient water heater uses only eight hundred to twelve hundred kilowatt hours of electricity a year compared to forty-five hundred to six thousand kilowatt hours for a standard model.

Lighting is another area in which individuals and businesses can use electricity more efficiently. Lighting in homes and businesses accounts for between 17 percent and 25 percent of the electric power used in the United States. Most people still use standard incandescent light bulbs for lighting. But 95 percent of the electricity used to power these bulbs is given off as waste heat instead of light. New energy-efficient bulbs use one-fourth to one-third the electricity of incandescent bulbs. Because energy-efficient bulbs and appliances use less electricity, less coal is needed to produce the electricity.

Reusing methane

Cutting back on greenhouse gas producers is one way of maintaining a balanced greenhouse effect. Reuse is another. Researchers have discovered ways of reusing methane rather than letting it escape into the air. Methane gas is the major component of natural gas and, like natural gas, it can be used as a fuel. One age-old source of methane, cow dung, produces the gas when it decomposes. Researchers have designed a way of converting methane gas from cow dung to fuel. They do this with biomass converters or digesters.

In many Third World countries, people burn the dried dung of cattle and other plant-eating animals for fuel. But the dung produces little heat, a lot of smoke, and a lot of carbon dioxide. Digesters use anaerobic bacteria to decompose dung and other farm debris. The methane produced by the bacteria is trapped so that it can be used for fuel.

In Masudpur, India, the dung produced by the village cattle is collected and decomposed in a community digester. The methane produced is piped into 140 homes for two hours in the morning and two in the evening for cooking meals and heating water. The sludge left over from the conversion process is sold for fertilizer.

These kinds of digesters could be used on farms that have as few as three or four cows or horses. They could be used by equestrian centers, cattle ranches, horse-racing tracks, and zoos to produce energy. The sludge could be used to fertilize gardens or crops.

This kind of fertilizing would also reduce the need to use chemical fertilizers. Switching from traditional farming to sustainable farming, where farmers manage pests, disease, and soil improvement by rotating crops in a certain order or by planting certain crops together, could also decrease the need for chemical fertilizers. That would decrease the amount of nitrous oxide going into the atmosphere.

Phasing out CFCs

CFCs are on their way out, too, although they will be around for a long time. In 1987, twenty-three nations signed the Montreal Protocol, an agreement that they would reduce their production of CFCs by half. Two years later, officials from eighty countries meeting in Helsinki, Finland, agreed to phase out CFCs by 2000. Until then, the gases will still be manufactured in those countries. CFCs will also be purchased and manufactured in countries that did not sign the agreement. This will continue to add to the greenhouse effect. There are still tons of CFCs in refrigerators, air conditioners, and insulation, too. They could be released into the atmosphere if they are not disposed of carefully when they have reached the end of their useful lives.

The re-greening of the world

In addition to preventing further greenhouse gas emissions, other actions can help remove those gases—primarily carbon dioxide—from the air. Because trees absorb tons of carbon dioxide from the atmosphere, they are an important tool for reducing the greenhouse effect.

In South America, groups of native peoples and others are trying to find substitutes for slash-and-burn practices that destroy trees and add to the imbalance in the greenhouse effect. In Acre, Brazil, for example, residents have created rain-forest reserves. Trees in the reserves are protected from logging and burning. Local people, however, collect fruits, nuts, oil, and rubber for sale in local, national, and international markets.

Workers in Paraguay prepare the ground for planting pine seedlings as part of a reforestation project.

Private and federal agencies are joining in the effort to plant new trees in Guatemala's vanishing rainforest.

Elsewhere, tree-planting has captured the imagination of people concerned about the greenhouse effect. Trees are a long-term solution to the increasing greenhouse effect. To absorb the next forty years' worth of carbon dioxide emissions, people would have to plant an area of land only slightly smaller than the area of the United States. Undaunted, many groups are going ahead with reforestation efforts anyway.

In the 1980s, Haiti was largely deforested. But a combination of private North American groups and Haitian groups got together and helped 135,000 farmers plant thirty-five million trees. Other groups raise money through various projects in order to buy and preserve rainforests in countries such as Costa Rica.

Applied Energy Services (AES), a small coal-burning power company, is engaged in a program that will, they estimate, at least remove the carbon dioxide their company puts into the air. The company maintains three electric power plants and is building five more. But it is helping forty thousand farmers plant fifty-two million trees in Guatemala's rainforest at a cost of $1.2 million. Another $2 million is coming from private and federal agencies in the United States and $1.2 million from the Guatemalan government. Over forty years, the trees, which will be planted by Peace Corps volunteers, will absorb an estimated fifteen million tons of carbon dioxide, the amount the company's plants are expected to produce.

Planting trees can help reduce the amount of carbon dioxide in the atmosphere in other ways as well, according to organizers of the Global Re-Leaf program. The group plans to plant 100 million trees which, they estimate, will absorb eighteen million tons of atmospheric carbon dioxide. That is less than 1 percent of the carbon dioxide in the atmosphere. However, the group reasons that if the trees were planted in cities, the cooling shade they provide might reduce the need people felt for air conditioning. Based on that assumption, they predict that planting city trees could mean a drop in air conditioner use and a reduction in the demand for power. That would also mean the emission of carbon dioxide from the power plants would fall. They estimate that 100 million trees planted in cities could save sixteen billion tons of coal and keep sixty million tons of carbon dioxide out of the atmosphere.

Taking the lead

Fundamental changes in energy sources, types of transportation, and life-style will be necessary to stem rising global temperatures due to an increased greenhouse effect, say many scientists. Many of those changes will be made—and some are already being made—by individuals and businesses. However, those who study the greenhouse effect say that without governmental leadership, those efforts will only help slightly. They urge members of governments around the world to take steps quickly to reduce the risk of global warming.

The leaders of many governments are beginning to listen as more and more scientists come to the conclusion that the greenhouse effect is increasing. Most industrialized nations, including France, Britain, Australia, Canada, and New Zealand, have long sought an international standard for reducing carbon dioxide emissions. One of the world's largest producers of carbon dioxide and other greenhouse gases, the United States, has been reluctant to support this standard.

Leaders in the United States have argued that efforts to reduce these gases are premature because there is no proof that global warming is caused by carbon dioxide, methane, and CFC emissions. They claim that the steps needed to reduce greenhouse gas emissions would be expen-

Chuck Asay, by permission of the *Colorado Springs Gazette Telegraph.*

sive and would cost jobs, hurting the nation's economy. Yet a 1991 report from the National Academy of Sciences, an organization of scientists and engineers that advises the U.S. government on subjects of science and technology, said the United States could reduce greenhouse gases by 40 percent with no harm to the economy. To reduce energy use and greenhouse gases, the academy recommended higher energy prices, energy-efficiency buildings, development of energy-efficient appliances and automobiles, the support

A report from the National Academy of Sciences advises the use of safe nuclear power as one way to reduce greenhouse gases.

of mass transit programs, the reduction of deforestation in the United States, and the development of safe nuclear power.

Although environmentalists in the United States have been disheartened by the lack of government leadership shown in the area of global warming, other countries are looking to the future. India, for example, is deeply committed to alternative forms of energy. The Indian government spends $60 million a year on renewable energy programs. India's Department of Non-Conventional Energy investigates and promotes the use of solar stoves, photovoltaics, wind farms, solar ponds, passive solar construction, and solar thermal power plants, all of which can help reduce the production of greenhouse gases. Even the building in which the department is housed is packed with alternative energy options, such as passive solar heating, extra insulation, fans, vents, windows to circulate the air, and natural lighting.

Earth Summit

Growing concern about the risk of global warming has prompted several international conferences on global warming and world climate since 1988. But the largest meeting to address the problem was the United Nations Conference on Environment and Development in June 1992 in Rio de Janeiro, Brazil. The conference, dubbed the Earth Summit, was attended by representatives from 178 countries.

Of the five documents discussed by members of the conference, two concern global warming. Agenda 21 is a complex plan to protect the environment throughout the world. Secretary General of the United Nations Boutros Boutros-Ghali called it the "centerpiece of international cooperation for years to come."

To address the problem of the greenhouse effect, Agenda 21 recommends steps for nations to take to cut energy use. It also provides for financial and technological aid for developing countries so that they can develop alternative fuels. Japan pledged $7.7 billion in aid; Germany, $6.3 billion; the European Community, $4 billion; and Great Britain, $2 to $3 billion. Agenda 21 is not legally binding. There is no way to guarantee that countries will live up to their promises.

The treaty that most directly affects the greenhouse effect is the Global Warming Convention. It calls for countries signing the agreement to develop programs to reduce the levels of greenhouse gases produced by human beings. To show that they are actively taking steps to reach lower emission levels, they must, within six months, report on what they have done about returning

Demonstrators during the Earth Summit international conference in Rio de Janeiro protest stands taken by the United States on certain environmental issues.

Higher water levels caused by global warming could potentially cover the Maldive Islands, which are only slightly above sea level.

greenhouse gas emissions to their 1990 levels. Treaty signatories must also pledge to protect forests that remove carbon dioxide from the atmosphere. The treaty also urges wealthier nations to provide financial and technological aid to developing countries.

Although early versions of the treaty contained emissions limits and target dates for achieving them, the final version does not. European countries wanted to require that emission levels be reduced to 1990 levels by 2000. However, the United States threatened it would not sign a treaty that specified emission levels and target dates. So those clauses were removed from the treaty. Although the Global Warming Convention is legally binding, without set emission levels or time frame for reducing greenhouse gases, the treaty's success may be limited.

Most conference members felt that the Earth Summit ended on a hopeful note, however. Individual governments must now ratify the treaties. Despite the compromises, many nations view the treaties and discussion as fruitful. Conference participants also urge nations and their citizens to be vigilant.

"People can't allow their leaders to forget what they promised here," said Maurice Strong, a former Canadian businessman who served as secretary general for the conference. For the risk to earth's inhabitants, such as those living in the Maldive Islands, is all too real.

The Maldive Islands in the Indian Ocean are little more than three feet above sea level. Higher water levels caused by global warming could completely cover the Maldives. The Maldives representative to the Earth Summit, Maumoon Abdul Gayoom, said, "We are a small nation and maybe our voice does not have weight. But do not let our voice go unheard, for if you do, it might be forever."

Glossary

albedo: The reflectivity of a planet or material, such as snow or ice.

anaerobic: Living or growing without atmospheric oxygen.

atmosphere: The odorless, tasteless, and invisible gases (air) that surround the earth.

chlorofluorocarbon (CFC): A group of gases that are combinations (compounds) of carbon, hydrogen, chlorine, and fluorine.

climate: The general range of weather conditions over a broad area.

combustion: Burning. A substance burns when it combines rapidly with oxygen giving off high heat and light. Combustion also takes place in body tissues as food is converted to energy. This kind of combustion produces low heat and no light.

deforestation: The removal of trees from the land.

fossil fuels: Burnable, fossilized, organic material, such as coal, oil, or natural gas.

fuel cell: A device that converts chemical energy from a fuel such as hydrogen directly and efficiently into electricity.

glacier: A large mass of ice that forms over many years because the amount of fallen snow is greater than the amount of snow that melts during the summer.

greenhouse effect: The absorbing and retaining of heat in the earth's atmosphere that results in higher temperatures on the earth's surface.

greenhouse gas: An atmospheric gas that traps and retains heat near the earth's surface. Carbon dioxide, methane, nitrous oxide, and water vapor are natural greenhouse gases. CFCs are human-made greenhouse gases.

ice age: Periods of geologic time when temperatures go down and ice, in the form of polar caps or glaciers, spreads over a large part of the world.

ice cap: A permanent area of ice covering large areas of land, particularly around the poles. An ice sheet.

ice sheet: An ice cap.

methane: A colorless, odorless gas composed of carbon and hydrogen.

natural gas: A fossil fuel made up primarily of methane, with ethane, butane, propane, and nitrogen.

nitrous oxide: A weak acid made up of two nitrogen atoms and one oxygen atom.

ozone: A molecule of three oxygen atoms. A layer of ozone in the upper part of the stratosphere (the upper part of the atmosphere) that protects the earth from the sun's damaging ultraviolet radiation.

permafrost: A layer of permanently frozen subsoil found in most of the Arctic. Permafrost may be as deep as nine hundred feet or more.

petroleum: A dark, oily, flammable, liquid hydrocarbon. Petroleum is a fossil fuel.

photosynthesis: The process by which plants use chlorophyll and light to create food from carbon dioxide and water. Photosynthesis releases oxygen into the atmosphere.

photovoltaic cell: A device made of different kinds of crystals that converts sunlight directly into electric current.

rainforest: A large, dense forest mostly made up of evergreen trees in an area of heavy, year-long rainfall. Most often, rainforests are in tropical regions, but they may also be found in temperate regions.

savannah: Grassland scattered with trees or shrubs that is often found in tropical or subtropical regions.

slash and burn: A method of clearing land that consists of cutting trees down and burning them.

ultraviolet radiation: A type of electromagnetic radiation with wavelengths longer than visible light but shorter than X rays. Too much exposure to UV radiation can cause sunburn and skin cancer.

wavelength: The distance between the top of one wave to the top of the next.

Suggestions for Further Reading

Sam Flamsteed, "H$_2$ OH!" *Discover*, February 1992.

Sam Flamsteed, "Star Spots," *Discover,* December 1991.

Michael Oppenheimer and Robert H. Boyle, *Dead Heat: The Race Against the Greenhouse Effect.* New York: Basic Books, Inc., 1990.

Stephen H. Schneider, *Global Warming: Are We Entering the Greenhouse Century?* San Francisco: Sierra Club Books, 1989.

James S. Trefil, "Modeling Earth's Future Climate Requires Both Science and Guesswork," *Smithsonian*, December 1990.

Works Consulted

Dean Edwin Abrahamson, ed., *The Challenge of Global Warming.* Washington, DC: Island Press, 1989.

Rudy Abramson, "Prompt Action to Curb Global Warming Urged," *Los Angeles Times*, April 11, 1991.

Rudy Abramson, "Talks on Global Warming Pact Could Put US in the Hot Seat," *Los Angeles Times,* February 3, 1991.

Neal Bernards, ed., *The Environmental Crisis: Opposing Viewpoints*. San Diego: Greenhaven Press, Inc., 1991.

David Berreby "Acid-Flecked Candy-Colored Sunscreen," *Discover*, January 1992.

Warren Brookes, "Sunspot Data Help Make Bush's Case," *Insight on the News*, December 16, 1991.

Discover, "Laughing Stock," November 1991.

David E. Fisher, *Fire and Ice: The Greenhouse Effect, Ozone Depletion, and Nuclear Winter*. New York: Harper and Row, 1990.

David Graham, "Scripps to Lead Study of Clouds, Global Warming," *San Diego Union*, December 9, 1991.

John Gribben, *Hothouse Earth: The Greenhouse Effect and Gaia*. New York: Grove Weidenfeld, 1990.

Robert Kunzig, "Earth on Ice," *Discover*, April 1991.

Los Angeles Times, "Dust From Mt. Pinatubo Eruption to Offset Global Warming Trend," August 14, 1991.

Bill McKibben, *The End of Nature*. New York: Random House, 1989.

Norman Myers, ed., *Gaia: An Atlas of Planet Management*. Garden City, NY: Anchor Press/Doubleday and Company, Inc., 1984.

Norman Myers, ed., "Trees by the Billions: A Blueprint for Cooling," *International Wildlife*, September/October 1991.

Rob Nicholson, "A Far Plateau," *Natural History*, September 1991.

Michael Parfit, "Antarctic Meltdown," *Discover*, September 1989.

Science News, "Antarctic Ice Potentially Unstable," May 5, 1990.

James Shreeve, "The Ice Man Cometh," *Discover*, January 1992.

Paul Wallich, "Murky Water: Just What Role Do Oceans Play in Absorbing Greenhouse Gases?" *Scientific American*, May 1990.

Index

About the Author

Sharon Elaine Thompson lives and writes in Salem, Oregon. She has been writing since 1985. She specializes in educational material but frequently writes articles about earth science, gemstones, wildlife, and history. This is her first book.

Picture Credits

Cover photo: FPG
American Recreation Coalition—Chevron Corp., 47
Courtesy American Petroleum Institute, 19, 31, 63
AP/Wide World Photos, 16, 54, 65
Bechtel Power Corp., 83
The Bettmann Archive, 50
Chevron Corp., 10
Courtesy Continental Oil Co., 29
Gamma Liaison, 44
© Greenpeace/Morgan, 85
Steve Kirk/© 1992 Discover Magazine, 55
Library of Congress, 22
Mary E. Messenger, 8
Benjamin Montag, 28
National Aeronautics and Space Administration, 12, 36, 40
Ohio State University, 18
Photri, 30, 59, 86
© Plowden 1989, Greenpeace, 27
Potomac Electrical Power Co., 53
© Thomas Raupach/Focus/Argus 1988, 75
Reuters/Bettmann, 38, 74
Solarex Corp., 72
Southern California Edison Co., 68
Sygma, 62
United Nations, 79
UPI/Bettman, 48, 67
UPI/Bettmann Newsphotos, 61
USDA—Soil Conservation Service, 70
U.S. Department of Interior, 14
© Eric Waterman, Greenpeace, 24, 80